Creatures of the Night

# Bobcats in the Dark

I0892212

By Therese Shea

Gareth Stevens Publishing

**Please visit our website, www.garethstevens.com. For a free color catalog of all our high-quality books, call toll free 1-800-542-2595 or fax 1-877-542-2596.**

**Library of Congress Cataloging-in-Publication Data**

Shea, Therese.
Bobcats in the dark / Therese Shea.
p. cm. — (Creatures of the night)
Includes index.
ISBN 978-1-4339-6366-7 (pbk.)
ISBN 978-1-4339-6367-4 (6-pack)
ISBN 978-1-4339-6364-3 (library binding)
1. Bobcat—Juvenile literature. 2. Nocturnal animals—Juvenile literature. I. Title.
QL737.C23S5318 2012
599.75'36—dc23
2011021349

First Edition

Published in 2013 by
**Gareth Stevens Publishing**
111 East 14th Street, Suite 349
New York, NY 10003



Designer: Daniel Hosek
Editor: Therese Shea

Photo credits: Cover, p. 1 Jeremy Woodhouse/Stockbyte/Getty Images; pp. 5, 7, 9, 15, 21 Shutterstock.com; pp. 11, 17 Thinkstock.com; p. 13 Alan and Sandy Carey/Getty Images; p. 19 Masterfile.com.



Printed in the United States of America

CPSIA compliance information: Batch #CW12GS: For further information contact Gareth Stevens, New York, New York at 1-800-542-2595.

# Contents



**Boldface** words appear in the glossary.

## How It Got Its Name

Did you ever wonder how the bobcat got its name? A bob is another name for a short haircut. This North American wildcat has a tail that looks like it was bobbed, or cut short. All bobcats have this bobbed, black-tipped tail.

## Big Kitty

Bobcats look a lot like house cats. They're about two times bigger. They have big, pointed ears with hair coming out of them. Their fur is mostly brown with dark spots or lines. They have a whitish belly.

## Where Are They?

There are more bobcats in North America than any other wildcat. However, they're hard to find. They like to stay away from people. They're usually **nocturnal**. They may come out on warm winter days.

Bobcats make their homes in Canada, the United States, and Mexico. They live in forests, mountains, and any place they can find a meal! They like areas with a lot of plants. Bobcats sometimes wait in trees and behind bushes for their **prey**.

## The Hunt

Bobcats are excellent hunters. To catch their prey, they creep up close . . . and leap! They can jump as far as 10 feet (3 m). Bobcats mostly eat small animals, such as rabbits. However, they sometimes hunt animals larger than themselves.

## At Home, All Alone

Bobcats like to be alone. They don't want to share meals. A bobcat marks its land with its **scent**. This tells other bobcats to stay away. A bobcat's area may be quite large. It may have more than one **den** there.

## Bobcat Kittens

When a mother bobcat is ready to have babies, she makes a hidden den. It might be under a log or in a tree. Mothers may have one kitten or as many as six. Kittens first open their eyes after about 10 days.

Bobcat kittens are furry and cute, but they grow up to be hunters! They stay with their mother for up to a year. At first, they drink milk from their mother. Then their mother brings them meat. Finally, she teaches them to hunt.

## Protecting Bobcats

Did you know that people hunt bobcats? Farmers kill them to **protect** their animals. Other people hunt bobcats for their fur. In some places, bobcats are protected from hunters. Today, there may be as many as a **million** wild bobcats.

## The Bobcat Fact Box

| | |
|---|---|
| **Length** | body, 26 to 41 inches (66 to 104 cm); tail, 4 to 7 inches (10 to 18 cm) |
| **Height** | 17 to 23 inches (43 to 58 cm) |
| **Weight** | up to 30 pounds (14 kg) |
| **Life span** | up to 13 years in the wild |

# Glossary

**den:** a wild animal's hidden home

**million:** a thousand thousands, or 1,000,000

**nocturnal:** active at night

**prey:** an animal that is hunted by other animals for food

**protect:** to guard

**scent:** a smell

# For More Information

## Books

Marks, Jennifer L. *Bobcats*. Mankato, MN: Capstone Press, 2011.

Randall, Henry. *Bobcats*. New York, NY: PowerKids Press, 2011.

Squire, Ann O. *Bobcats*. New York, NY: Children's Press, 2005.

## Websites

**Bobcat**
*animals.nationalgeographic.com/animals/mammals/bobcat/*
Read about bobcats, and hear what they sound like.

**Bobcat: Lynx rufus**
*www.defenders.org/wildlife_and_habitat/wildlife/bobcat.php*
Find out much more about bobcats and how people are working to protect them.

**Publisher's note to educators and parents:** Our editors have carefully reviewed these websites to ensure that they are suitable for students. Many websites change frequently, however, and we cannot guarantee that a site's future contents will continue to meet our high standards of quality and educational value. Be advised that students should be closely supervised whenever they access the Internet.

# Index